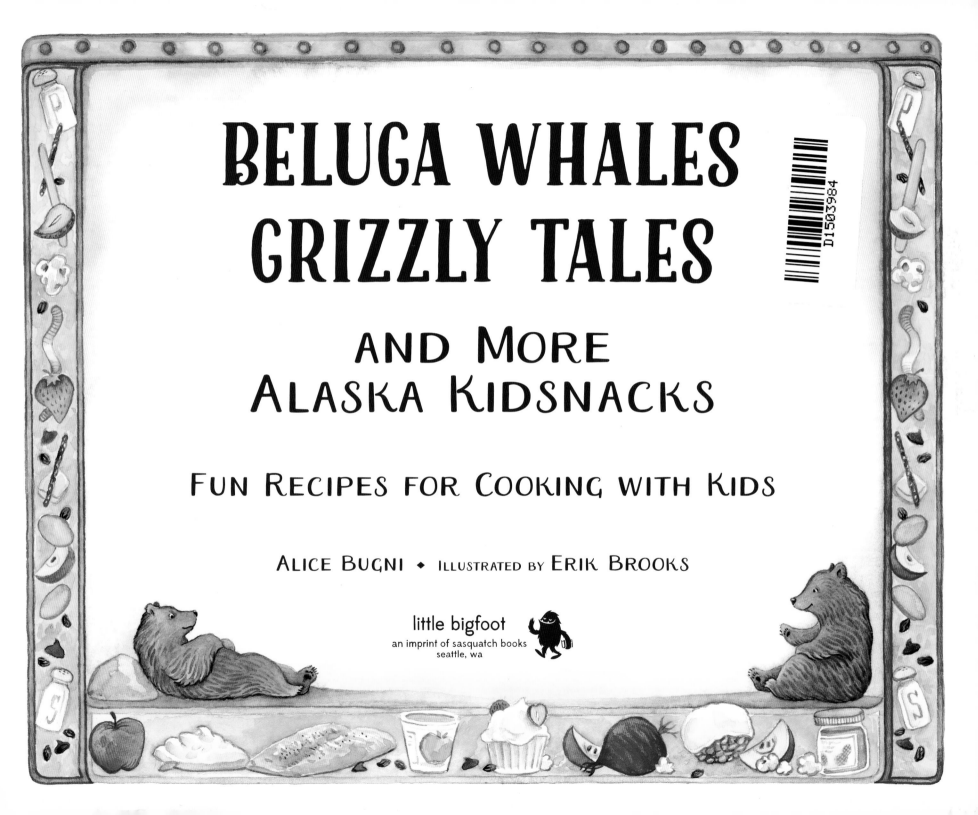

BELUGA WHALES
GRIZZLY TALES

AND MORE
ALASKA KIDSNACKS

FUN RECIPES FOR COOKING WITH KIDS

ALICE BUGNI ◆ ILLUSTRATED BY ERIK BROOKS

little bigfoot
an imprint of sasquatch books
seattle, wa

Manufactured in China by Midas Printing International Ltd. (Hong Kong), in November 2015

Published by Little Bigfoot, an imprint of Sasquatch Books
20 19 18 17 16   9 8 7 6 5 4 3 2 1

Editors: Tegan Tigani and Christy Cox
Production editor: Emma Reh
Design: Anna Goldstein

Library of Congress Cataloging-in-Publication Data is available.
ISBN: 978-1-57061-999-1
Sasquatch Books
1904 Third Avenue, Suite 710
Seattle, WA 98101
(206) 467-4300
www.sasquatchbooks.com
custserv@sasquatchbooks.com

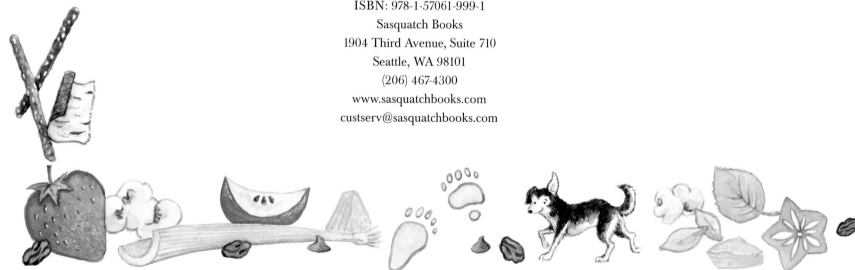

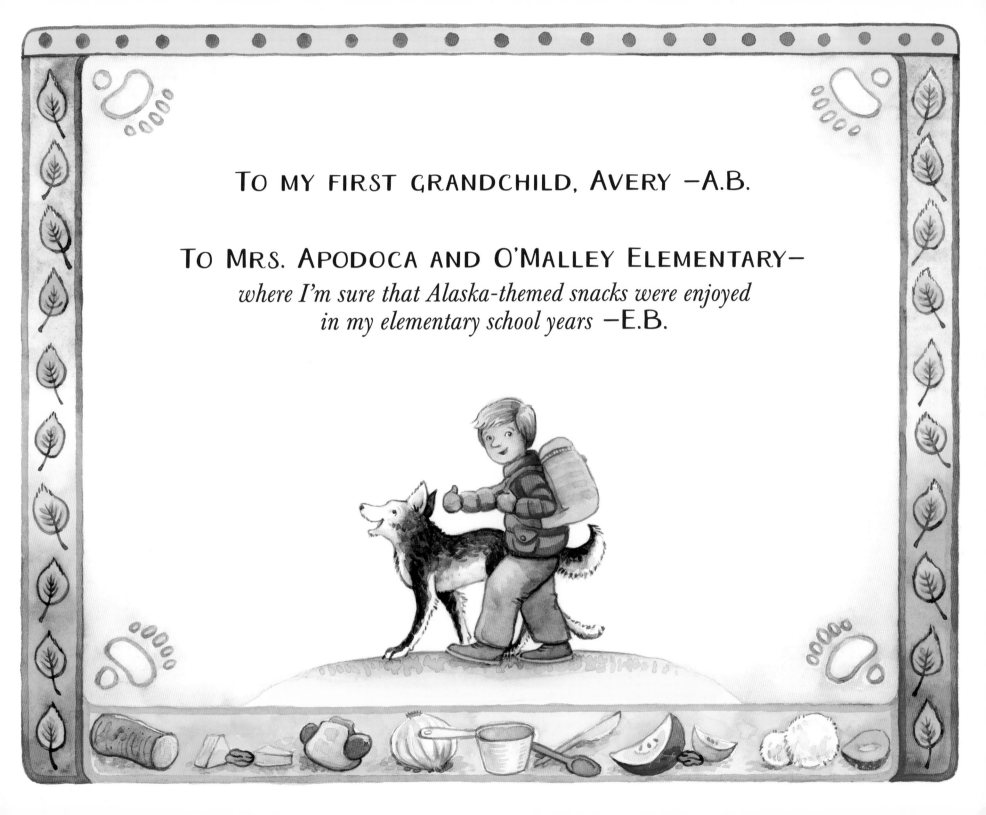

To my first grandchild, Avery —A.B.

To Mrs. Apodoca and O'Malley Elementary—
*where I'm sure that Alaska-themed snacks were enjoyed
in my elementary school years* —E.B.

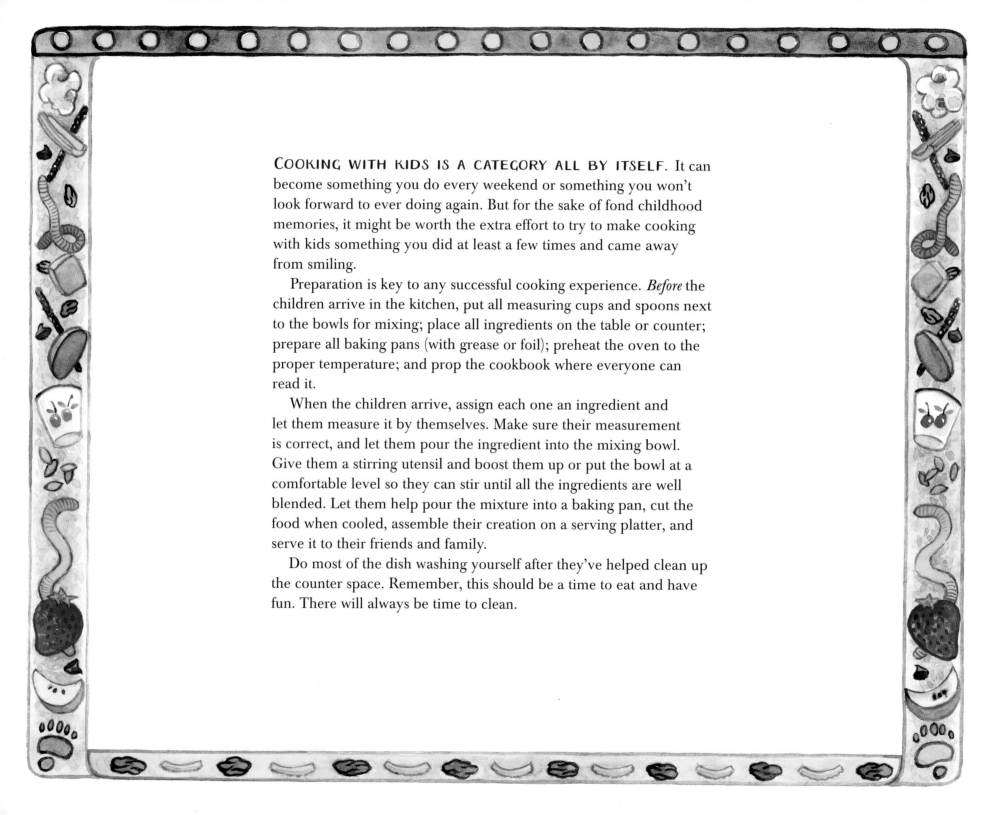

COOKING WITH KIDS IS A CATEGORY ALL BY ITSELF. It can become something you do every weekend or something you won't look forward to ever doing again. But for the sake of fond childhood memories, it might be worth the extra effort to try to make cooking with kids something you did at least a few times and came away from smiling.

Preparation is key to any successful cooking experience. *Before* the children arrive in the kitchen, put all measuring cups and spoons next to the bowls for mixing; place all ingredients on the table or counter; prepare all baking pans (with grease or foil); preheat the oven to the proper temperature; and prop the cookbook where everyone can read it.

When the children arrive, assign each one an ingredient and let them measure it by themselves. Make sure their measurement is correct, and let them pour the ingredient into the mixing bowl. Give them a stirring utensil and boost them up or put the bowl at a comfortable level so they can stir until all the ingredients are well blended. Let them help pour the mixture into a baking pan, cut the food when cooled, assemble their creation on a serving platter, and serve it to their friends and family.

Do most of the dish washing yourself after they've helped clean up the counter space. Remember, this should be a time to eat and have fun. There will always be time to clean.

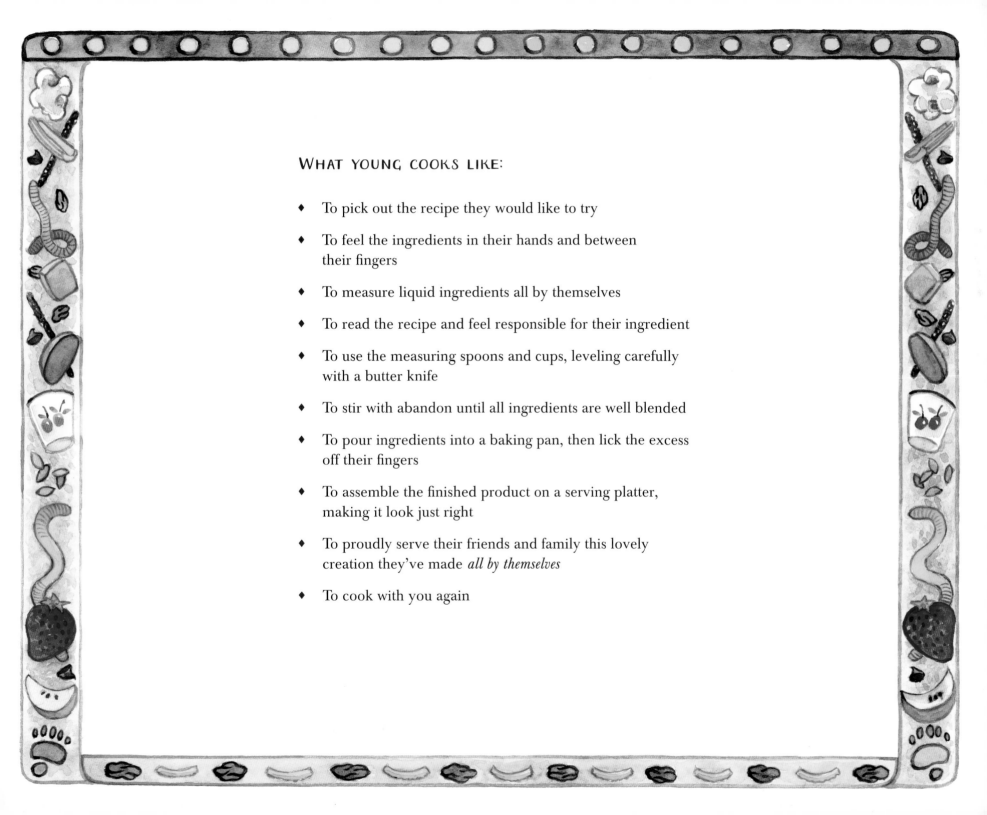

WHAT YOUNG COOKS LIKE:

- ♦ To pick out the recipe they would like to try

- ♦ To feel the ingredients in their hands and between their fingers

- ♦ To measure liquid ingredients all by themselves

- ♦ To read the recipe and feel responsible for their ingredient

- ♦ To use the measuring spoons and cups, leveling carefully with a butter knife

- ♦ To stir with abandon until all ingredients are well blended

- ♦ To pour ingredients into a baking pan, then lick the excess off their fingers

- ♦ To assemble the finished product on a serving platter, making it look just right

- ♦ To proudly serve their friends and family this lovely creation they've made *all by themselves*

- ♦ To cook with you again

CONTENTS

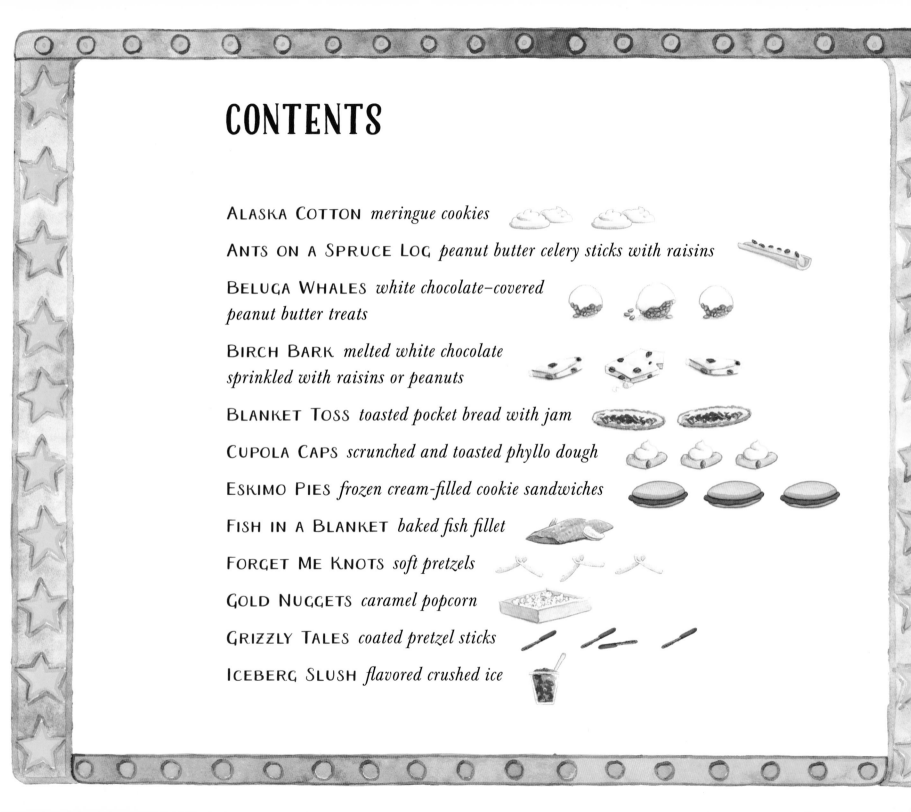

HOT LAVA *applesauce*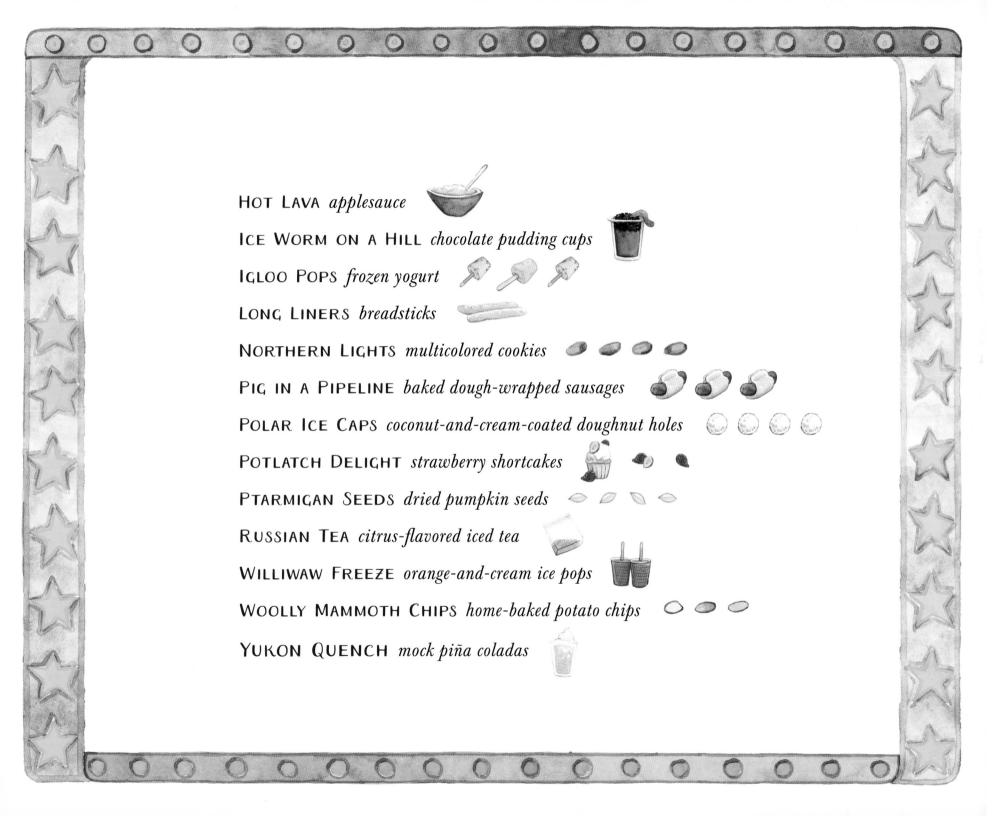

ICE WORM ON A HILL *chocolate pudding cups*

IGLOO POPS *frozen yogurt*

LONG LINERS *breadsticks*

NORTHERN LIGHTS *multicolored cookies*

PIG IN A PIPELINE *baked dough-wrapped sausages*

POLAR ICE CAPS *coconut-and-cream-coated doughnut holes*

POTLATCH DELIGHT *strawberry shortcakes*

PTARMIGAN SEEDS *dried pumpkin seeds*

RUSSIAN TEA *citrus-flavored iced tea*

WILLIWAW FREEZE *orange-and-cream ice pops*

WOOLLY MAMMOTH CHIPS *home-baked potato chips*

YUKON QUENCH *mock piña coladas*

ALASKA COTTON

2 egg whites

⅛ teaspoon cream of tartar

⅛ teaspoon kosher salt

¾ cup superfine sugar

1 teaspoon vanilla extract

Preheat the oven to 225 degrees F. Grease a cookie sheet and set aside.

In a medium bowl, using an electric mixer, beat the egg whites, cream of tartar, and salt until soft peaks form, about 5 minutes. Slowly stir in the sugar. Add the vanilla and beat until the mixture is stiff.

Dollop teaspoonfuls of the batter onto the prepared cookie sheet, and bake for 20 to 30 minutes, or until the bottoms of the cookies are lightly browned. Cookies will be chewy on the inside.

MAKES ABOUT 3 DOZEN COOKIES

Cotton-like flowers flourish in wet bogs and tundra;
roadside ditches; peaty soil; and warm, shallow water.

ANTS ON A SPRUCE LOG

8 celery stalks
1 cup peanut butter
½ cup raisins

Trim the ends of each celery stalk, rinse, and pat dry. Cut each stalk in half or into thirds, and use a butter knife to spread the peanut butter down the center of each stalk. Sprinkle the stalks with the raisins.

MAKES 16 TO 24 LOGS

Scurrying busily inside uprooted trees,
ants become bear food during lazy summer days.

BELUGA WHALES

1 cup peanut butter
½ cup corn syrup
1 cup crispy rice cereal
2 cups white chocolate chips

Line a cookie sheet with foil and set aside.

In a large bowl, stir the peanut butter and corn syrup together, until blended. Add the cereal, and use your hands to combine. Shape the mixture into 1½-inch-diameter balls, and place on the prepared cookie sheet. Refrigerate for 2 hours, or until firm.

Put the chocolate chips into a microwave-safe bowl, and microwave on low power in 10-second increments, stirring the chocolate well between each increment, until the chocolate has melted. Dip the chilled peanut butter balls into the melted chocolate, and place them back on the cookie sheet. Refrigerate for another 20 minutes, or until the chocolate has hardened.

MAKES 1 DOZEN TREATS

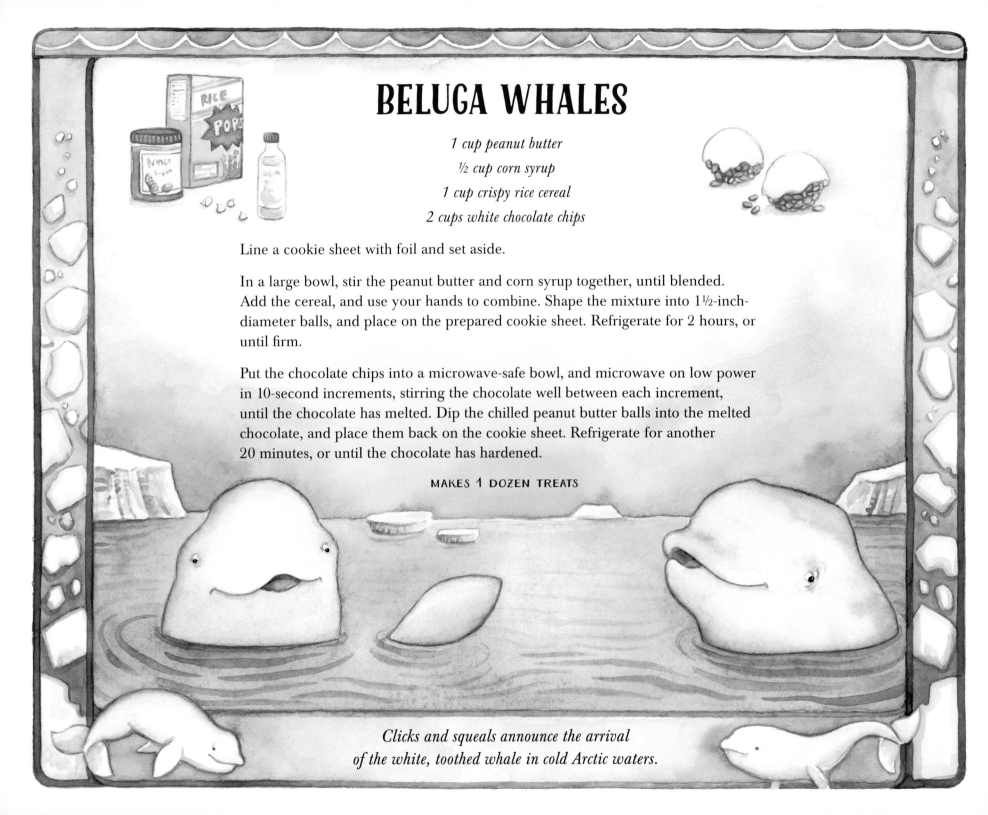

*Clicks and squeals announce the arrival
of the white, toothed whale in cold Arctic waters.*

BIRCH BARK

1 (14-ounce) can sweetened condensed milk

3 cups white chocolate chips

1 teaspoon vanilla extract

½ cup raisins or crushed peanuts

Line a 13-by-9-inch baking dish with waxed paper and set aside.

In a saucepan over low heat, melt the condensed milk and chocolate chips, stirring continuously. Slowly stir in the vanilla, remove the pan from the heat, and add the raisins. Pour mixture into the prepared baking dish, and refrigerate for 2 hours.

Lift the bark out of the pan, remove the waxed paper, and cut into pieces.

MAKES 2 POUNDS BARK

Amidst a stand of willowy trees,
a breeze makes music with rustling leaves.

BLANKET TOSS

6 pieces of pocket or pita bread

½ cup butter or margarine

1 cup preserves, jelly, or jam

Preheat the oven to 425 degrees F.

Lay the pocket bread flat on a cutting board, and slice each piece horizontally so that you end with 12 round pieces of bread. Spread the butter on the rough side of each piece of bread. Place on a cookie sheet, butter side up, and bake for 4 minutes, until the bread is crisp. Let the bread cool, and spread the preserves on the bread.

MAKES 1 DOZEN PIECES

A walrus-hide blanket grasped in a wide circle
tossed hunters up high to spot game and to mingle.

CUPOLA CAPS

¼ cup granulated sugar

1 teaspoon ground cinnamon

5 (9-by-14-inch) sheets phyllo dough, thawed

Vegetable oil spray

Whipped cream, for serving

Preheat the oven to 350 degrees F. Lightly grease a cookie sheet and set aside.

In a small bowl, combine the sugar and cinnamon, and set aside. Carefully lay one sheet of phyllo dough on a clean surface, and cover the remaining sheets with a damp paper towel or cloth to keep them from drying out. Spray one side of the sheet with the oil spray, and sprinkle with the cinnamon-sugar mix. Cut the sheet into 6 even pieces. Very carefully fold the sides of each piece toward the center, and using your hands, very gently round the corners and flatten slightly. Repeat this process with the remaining sheets of phyllo dough. Place the caps on the prepared cookie sheet and bake for 15 minutes, or until the caps are lightly browned. Top each cap with a dollop of the whipped cream.

MAKES 30 CAPS

Adorning the tops of Russian cathedrals,
cross-bearing domes provide light and decoration.

ESKIMO PIES

1½ cups whole milk

1 (3.9-ounce) box instant chocolate pudding mix

½ cup peanut butter

1 (11-ounce) box chocolate or vanilla wafer cookies

In a medium bowl, whisk together the milk and pudding, and set aside for 5 minutes. Add the peanut butter, stirring until blended. Sandwich two wafer cookies with 1 tablespoon of the pudding mixture. Place the sandwiches on a cookie sheet and freeze for 1 hour, or until firm.

MAKES ABOUT 30 PIES

Watertight boots, trousers, and parkas are worn by the Inuit ("the real people") of Alaska's far north.

FISH IN A BLANKET

1 (6-ounce) fresh salmon or halibut fillet
Kosher salt and freshly ground black pepper
1 tablespoon extra-virgin olive oil
½ onion, cut into rings

Preheat the oven to 425 degrees F.

Clean and rinse the fillet, and place it in the middle of a 12-by-12-inch piece of aluminum foil. Season to taste with the salt and pepper, drizzle with the oil, and top with the onion. Pinch the edges of foil tightly together to seal in the fillet. Place it on a cookie sheet and bake for 15 to 20 minutes, or until the fish flakes easily with a fork.

MAKES 1 TO 2 SERVINGS

Chinook, Sockeye, Coho, and Humpy
return to Alaska during warm summer weather.

FORGET ME KNOTS

2 cups hot water

2 tablespoons baking soda

1 (16.3-ounce) tube refrigerated breadstick dough

Coarse salt

Cheese sauce or mustard, for serving (optional)

Preheat the oven to 400 degrees F. Line an ungreased cookie sheet with foil and set aside.

In a medium bowl, combine the water and baking soda, and set aside. Remove the dough from the tube and separate each breadstick. To form one knot, cross 2 breadsticks at their ends and pinch to seal. Dip the knot briefly in the baking soda water, place on the prepared cookie sheet, and sprinkle with the salt. Bake for 7 minutes, or until lightly browned. Serve with cheese sauce or mustard.

MAKES 4 BREADSTICK KNOTS

Alaska's state flower sits perched on a stem
in a cluster of blue petals, near slow-moving streams.

GOLD NUGGETS

8 cups popped popcorn
½ cup butter
1 cup packed brown sugar
¼ cup corn syrup
½ teaspoon kosher salt
½ teaspoon vanilla extract
¼ teaspoon baking soda

Preheat the oven to 250 degrees F. Grease a large cookie sheet and set aside.

Put the popcorn in a large bowl and set aside. In a 2-quart saucepan over low heat, melt the butter. Stir in the sugar, corn syrup, and salt. Increase the heat to medium-low and boil for 5 minutes, without stirring. Remove the saucepan from the heat, and stir in the vanilla and baking soda. Pour the sugar mixture over the popcorn and stir until every piece is moistened. Spread the popcorn mixture onto the prepared cookie sheet and bake for 1 hour, stirring every 15 minutes.

MAKES 8 CUPS POPCORN

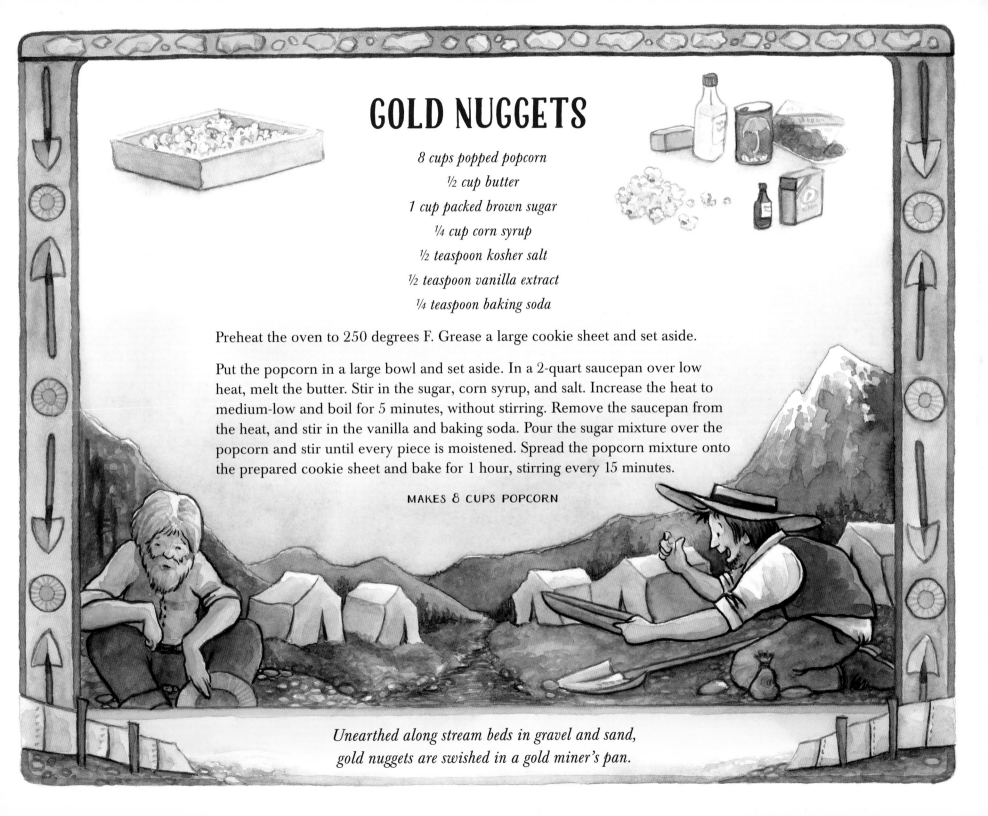

Unearthed along stream beds in gravel and sand,
gold nuggets are swished in a gold miner's pan.

GRIZZLY TALES

Assorted cake-decorating sprinkles
1 (8-ounce) container semisweet dipping chocolate
1 (12-ounce) package pretzel sticks

Line a cookie sheet with waxed paper and set aside.

Place the sprinkles into a bowl or container with a wide mouth and set aside. Using the directions on the package, melt the dipping chocolate. Dip one end of each pretzel in the chocolate, dip it in the sprinkles, and place it on the prepared cookie sheet. Refrigerate the pretzels for 20 minutes, or until the chocolate has hardened.

MAKES ABOUT 2 DOZEN PRETZELS

Sitting around a campfire late at night,
telling tales about grizzlies can cause a great fright.

ICEBERG SLUSH

1 teaspoon unflavored gelatin

1 tablespoon cold water

1 cup frozen strawberries, thawed

1 cup lemon-lime soda pop

In a small bowl, dissolve the gelatin in the water, and set aside. In a blender, puree the strawberries. Add the gelatin mixture to the blender and blend until smooth. Slowly add the soda pop to the strawberry mixture. Pour the slush into a 1-quart ziplock bag, and freeze for at least 4 to 5 hours or up to overnight.

MAKES 2 CUPS SLUSH

*Into glacier-fed salt water and freshwater lakes,
boulders of ice crash and drift slowly away.*

HOT LAVA

4 red apples, cored, peeled, and chopped into pieces

¾ cup apple cider, or enough to cover the apples

2 tablespoons corn syrup

½ teaspoon pumpkin pie spice or cinnamon

In a medium saucepan over medium-low heat, combine all the ingredients. Cover and simmer until apples are soft, about 15 to 20 minutes. Remove the saucepan from the heat and allow the mixture to cool. Once the apples are cool, mash them with a fork or a potato masher.

MAKES ABOUT 4 CUPS APPLESAUCE

Katmai National Monument, "The Valley of 10,000 Smokes":
a volcanic legacy in a wilderness so remote.

ICE WORM ON A HILL

3 cups whole milk
1 (5.9-ounce) box instant chocolate pudding mix
8 (5-ounce) plastic cups
8 chocolate wafer cookies, crushed
8 gummy worms

In a lidded 2-quart container, combine the milk and pudding mix and shake vigorously for 40 seconds, or stir with a whisk for 1 minute. Quickly pour the pudding into the plastic cups, filling them about two-thirds full. Sprinkle each cup with the crushed cookies and place one gummy worm into each cup. Refrigerate until ready to serve.

MAKES 8 SERVINGS

Marching down Main Street in a town called Cordova,
a festival commemorates this shy glacier dweller.

IGLOO POPS

6 (6-ounce) honey or vanilla yogurt cups
¾ cup diced fresh fruit, fruit preserves, or jam
6 flat wooden ice pop sticks

Remove yogurt cup lids and stir 2 tablespoons of the fruit into each cup, until well blended. Place an ice pop stick into each cup, put the cups in the freezer, and freeze for 4 to 5 hours, or overnight.

MAKES 6 POPS

A frigid dwelling made of compact snow
has icy windows and a small airhole.

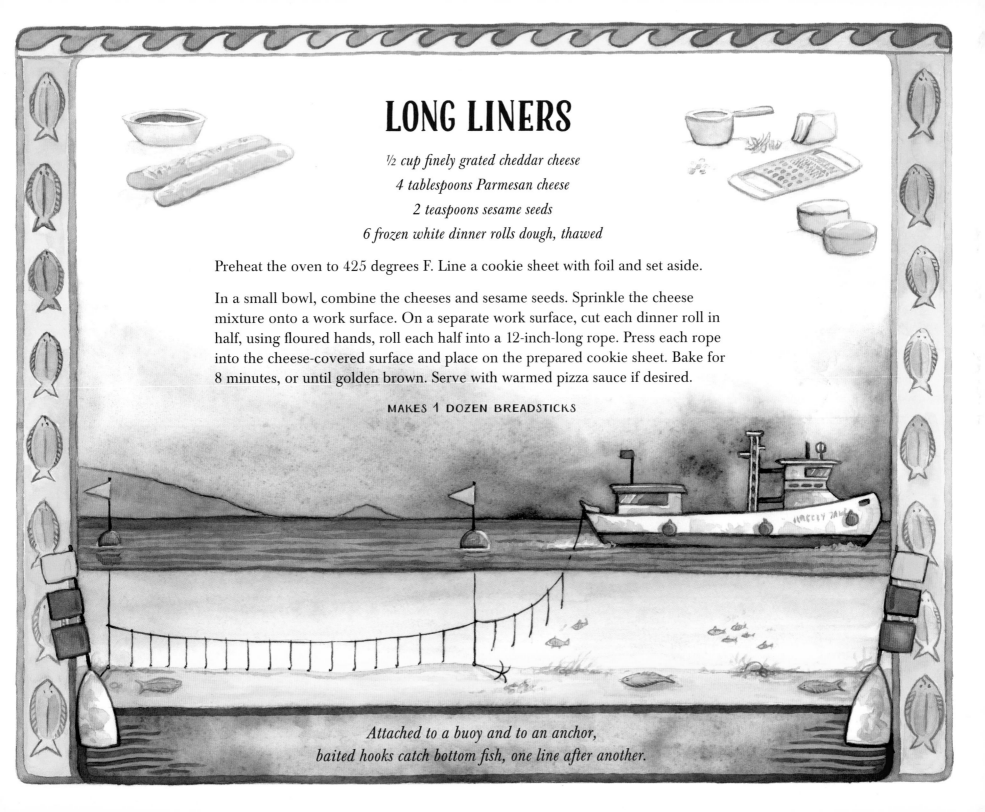

LONG LINERS

½ cup finely grated cheddar cheese
4 tablespoons Parmesan cheese
2 teaspoons sesame seeds
6 frozen white dinner rolls dough, thawed

Preheat the oven to 425 degrees F. Line a cookie sheet with foil and set aside.

In a small bowl, combine the cheeses and sesame seeds. Sprinkle the cheese mixture onto a work surface. On a separate work surface, cut each dinner roll in half, using floured hands, roll each half into a 12-inch-long rope. Press each rope into the cheese-covered surface and place on the prepared cookie sheet. Bake for 8 minutes, or until golden brown. Serve with warmed pizza sauce if desired.

MAKES 1 DOZEN BREADSTICKS

Attached to a buoy and to an anchor,
baited hooks catch bottom fish, one line after another.

NORTHERN LIGHTS

1 (16.5-ounce) tube refrigerated sugar cookie dough, room temperature
6 drops red food coloring
6 drops yellow food coloring
6 drops green food coloring

Preheat the oven to 350 degrees F. Line a cookie sheet with foil, and set aside.

Cut the cookie dough into three equal balls. Poke a hole in one of the balls of dough, and drip in the red food coloring. Repeat with the yellow and green food coloring and the other two balls of dough. Knead each ball of dough until color is well distributed. Form multicolored balls by combining 1 teaspoon of each color. Flatten the balls and place them on the prepared cookie sheet. Bake for 6 to 10 minutes.

MAKES 2 DOZEN COOKIES

Aurora borealis light shows fill the night sky
with dim-colored light beams that twist, soar, and fly.

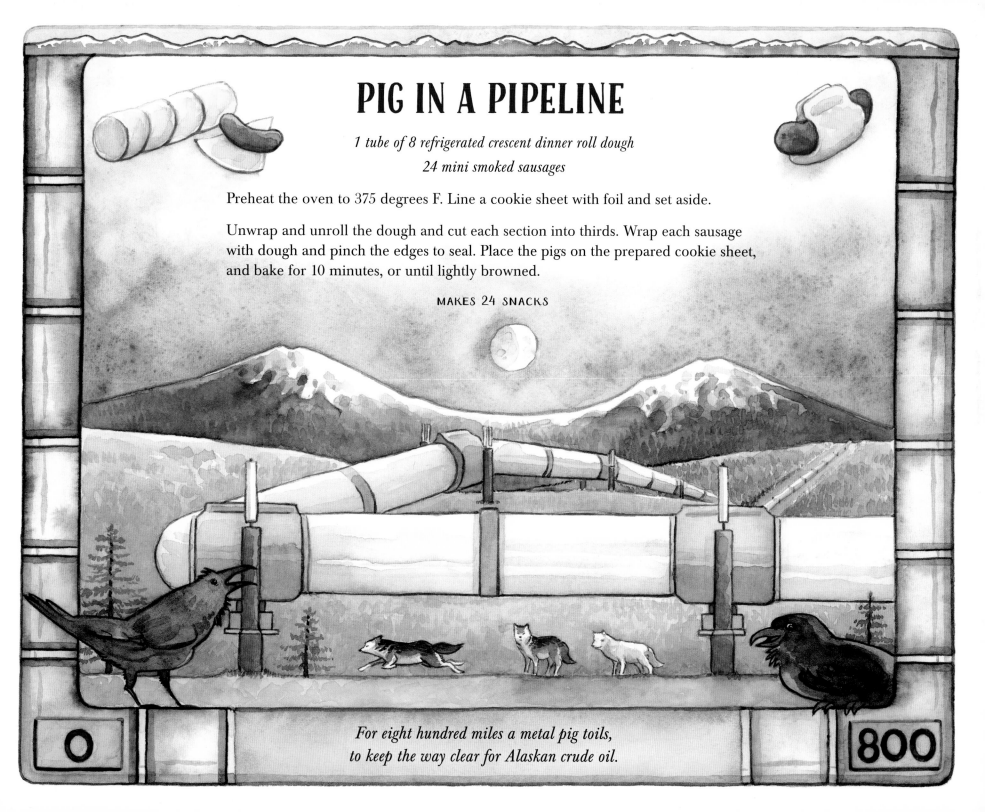

PIG IN A PIPELINE

1 tube of 8 refrigerated crescent dinner roll dough
24 mini smoked sausages

Preheat the oven to 375 degrees F. Line a cookie sheet with foil and set aside.

Unwrap and unroll the dough and cut each section into thirds. Wrap each sausage with dough and pinch the edges to seal. Place the pigs on the prepared cookie sheet, and bake for 10 minutes, or until lightly browned.

MAKES 24 SNACKS

For eight hundred miles a metal pig toils,
to keep the way clear for Alaskan crude oil.

POLAR ICE CAPS

1 (14-ounce) package shredded coconut
4 (3.25-ounce) ready-to-eat vanilla pudding cups
1 (8-ounce) container whipped cream topping
36 plain doughnut holes (about 1 pound)

Line a cookie sheet with foil, and set aside.

Put the coconut into a shallow dish and set aside. In a large bowl, stir together the pudding and whipped cream topping until well blended. Dip doughnut holes into the pudding mixture, coating them thoroughly. Roll the doughnut holes in the coconut to lightly coat, place them on the prepared cookie sheet, and freeze for 1 hour to harden.

MAKES 3 DOZEN CAPS

The snow-covered Arctic is like a dry desert,
and the Antarctic has the coldest-ever recorded climate.

POTLATCH DELIGHT

1 (16-ounce) box pound-cake mix, plus ingredients on cake-mix box
Whipped cream topping, for serving
1 pint fresh strawberries, sliced, for serving

Using the instructions on the cake-mix box, make the pound-cake cupcakes. After the cupcakes have cooled, arrange them on individual serving plates, and top each with the whipped cream topping and strawberries.

MAKES 2 DOZEN CUPCAKES

Native customs commemorate important events
with food and gifts, spirited songs, and dance.

PTARMIGAN SEEDS

1 tablespoon butter, melted

¼ teaspoon celery salt

⅛ teaspoon garlic powder

1 cup raw pumpkin seeds

⅛ teaspoon kosher salt

Preheat the oven to 350 degrees F. Line a cookie sheet with foil, and set aside.

In a medium bowl, combine the butter, celery salt, and garlic powder. Add the pumpkin seeds and toss until evenly coated. Spread the seeds evenly on the prepared cookie sheet, sprinkle with the salt, and bake for 20 minutes, rotating the cookie sheet halfway through.

MAKES 1 CUP SEEDS

Alaska's state bird thrives on tundras and moors,
eating seeds and leaves and berries galore.

RUSSIAN TEA

2 cups Tang mix

½ cup unsweetened iced tea mix

½ cup lemon-flavored iced tea mix

1 teaspoon ground cinnamon

½ teaspoon ground cloves

½ teaspoon ground allspice

Combine all the ingredients in a ziplock bag and shake gently until blended. Store in a lidded jar. To serve, mix 2 tablespoons of the Russian Tea mix with 1 cup hot water.

MAKES ABOUT 20 SERVINGS

Samovars of ornate and intricate design
serve tea made with cinnamon and sliced orange rind.

WILLIWAW FREEZE

1 (3.4-ounce) box instant vanilla pudding mix
2 cups orange juice
1 (8-ounce) container whipped cream topping
10 (5-ounce) plastic cups
10 flat wooden ice pop sticks

In a lidded 2-quart container, combine the pudding mix and orange juice and shake vigorously for 2 minutes. Add the whipped cream and shake for an additional 30 seconds. Pour evenly into the plastic cups, insert an ice pop stick into each cup, and freeze for 6 hours or overnight.

MAKES 10 ICE POPS

A sudden gust of enormous wind
builds up and spills over high mountain bends.

WOOLLY MAMMOTH CHIPS

1 large baking potato, sweet potato, or red beet
1 tablespoon vegetable oil
1 teaspoon onion salt

Preheat the oven to 375 degrees. Line a cookie sheet with foil and set aside.

Clean the potato, pat it dry, and cut it into ¼- to ½-inch slices. In a medium bowl, toss the potato slices in the oil and onion salt until evenly coated. Place the potato slices on the prepared cookie sheet, and bake for 15 to 25 minutes. Halfway through baking, turn the slices over and rotate the cookie sheet.

MAKES 2 TO 3 SERVINGS

Sporting a trunk, thick hair, and long tusks,
Ice Age mammoths roamed across ancient, wide steppes.

YUKON QUENCH

1 (8-ounce) can crushed pineapple, chilled

⅓ cup cream of coconut

2 cups coarsely crushed ice

Whipped cream topping, for serving

In a blender, blend the pineapple, cream of coconut, and ice until smooth, about 1 minute. Pour into serving glasses and top with whipped cream.

MAKES 4 SERVINGS

Across Alaska the Yukon River flows,
from east to west, through parts unknown.